Dorset

Stretching from the elegant Georgian town of Lyme Regis in the w... Bournemouth in the east, Dorset has a rich diversity of attractions. Where the chalk downland meets the sea, the impressive Jurassic Coast has long been a popular hunting ground for fossil collectors. The coastline is indented with sandy coves and fine beaches, and in many places the cliffs have been carved into dramatic shapes by the relentless action of the wind and sea. Inland is the timeless heathland and pastoral scenery which Thomas Hardy portrayed so vividly in his novels. Historic market towns and ancient villages testify to the rich heritage of the county which is also famous for its prehistoric earthworks and intriguing figures carved in the chalk hillsides.

Isle of Purbeck

Dominated by the majestic ruins of its castle, the village of **Corfe Castle** (*above*) is largely built of local grey Purbeck stone. This ancient site was probably first fortified by King Alfred as a defence against the Danes, but the present castle, situated strategically in a gap in the Purbeck Hills, was originally a Norman structure. One of the most impressive ruins in southern England, it was rebuilt in the 15th century and had six towers in addition to the two which flank the Gate House. Roundhead forces besieged the castle during the Civil War, after which it was largely demolished, much of the stone being taken to build houses in the village. The road from Corfe to Wareham crosses the open, sandy expanse of Wareham Heath where the **Blue Pool** (*right*), surrounded by pine trees, has been declared a Site of Special Scientific Interest because of its varied animal and plant life. The pool occupies the site of an old clay pit and it is the residual clay particles which give the water its remarkable intensity of colour.

To the east of Corfe Castle a road leads out to **Studland** (*bottom*), a pretty village set in a secluded bay close to the sea, downs and woods. At the southern end of the bay is the spit of land called The Foreland, off which stand the chalk stacks known as **Old Harry Rocks** (*top*). These prominent landmarks have been eroded over the years by the action of the wind and waves. The delightful old town of **Wareham** (*right*) is a popular centre for fishermen and small-boat enthusiasts. Overlooking the quay is St. Mary's Church which contains the marble coffin of Edward the Martyr who died in 978 AD. An important settlement in Saxon times, Wareham suffered at the hands of the Danes and again during the Civil War.

Once it was no more than a little fishing village, but **Swanage** has now grown into a popular seaside resort with safe bathing and good anchorage for yachts. Sheltered to the north by the high chalk cliffs of Ballard Down, the town lies at the southern end of a semicircular sandy bay. There are many reminders of the old part of the town, particularly in the area around the Mill Pond (*left*) which is surrounded by attractive stone-built cottages and overlooked by the church with its sturdy 13th century tower. The Great Globe (*bottom*) stands in the Durlston Country Park just south of the town. One of the outstanding attractions of the area, it weighs 40 tons and is 10 feet in diameter. Although built from huge blocks of local stone, the globe was constructed in London, in fifteen separate sections, and reassembled on site in the 1880s.

Beautiful **Kimmeridge Bay** (*right*) lies some five miles south-west of Corfe Castle. At one time this unspoiled but accessible cove was associated with smugglers. On the cliff-top stands Clavell Tower, a folly built in the 1820s by the Rev. John Clavell. It overlooks a shingle beach broken by rocky

ledges which provide a rich habitat for marine life. **Chapman's Pool** (*below*) is a lonely cove situated at the foot of St. Aldhelm's Head and backed by sombre cliffs which are dark in colour due to the presence of Kimmeridge clay. The beach can be reached by a path which follows an old river valley down the cliffs. In past centuries this rocky coastline caused many shipwrecks, but today it is visited by fishermen and geologists who find a rich source of fossil evidence in the area.

Situated on the hills behind Swanage, **Worth Matravers** (*left*) was once a busy stone-quarrying village. A number of ancient cottages are clustered around the village pond, and there is also an interesting church which dates from Saxon times with Norman additions.

The chalk downs meet the sea at Lulworth in an impressive stretch of coastline where the high white cliffs are indented with sandy coves. **Lulworth Cove** (*above*), one of England's most photographed spots, is nearly circular in shape. The power of the waves breaking into **Stair Hole** (*below*) are gradually carving out a second cove beside Lulworth. West of the famous cove is **Durdle Door** (*left*), a spectacular natural arch of rock which was created by the action of the sea over a period of time wearing away soft rock to leave an arch of harder Portland stone.

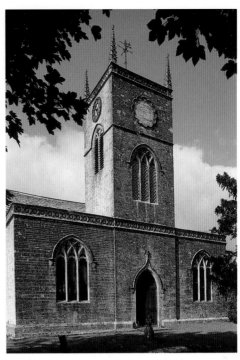

The heathland of central Dorset features in the novels of Thomas Hardy and is studded with quiet little villages which have changed little since he wrote about them. T. E. Lawrence, better known as "Lawrence of Arabia", bought **Clouds Hill** (*above*) as a retreat in 1925. Situated between Wareham and Dorchester, the gamekeeper's cottage which he called "an earthly paradise" is now owned by The National Trust. The village of **Moreton**, with its picturesque thatched cottages, is also associated with Lawrence, who was killed in a motor-cycle accident in 1935 and is buried in the churchyard of the beautiful little Church of St. Nicholas (*right*). The delightful village of **Wool** (*below*) stands on the River Frome, surrounded by water meadows and heathland. The 17th century bridge which spans the river is one of the finest in the county, and bears a rare transportation tablet threatening deportation as the penalty for misdemeanours such as driving an overloaded cart across the bridge. Elizabethan Woolbridge Manor was used by Thomas Hardy in *Tess of the D'Urbervilles* as the setting for the wedding night of Tess and Angel Clare.

Around Dorchester

Featuring as Casterbridge in Thomas Hardy's novels, **Dorchester** (*right*) is still a bustling market town. A number of interesting old buildings can be seen in High West Street, including the Old Crown Court where the trial of the Tolpuddle Martyrs took place in 1834 and the impressive Tudor building where the infamous Judge Jeffreys lodged when he held the "Bloody Assizes" following the defeat of Monmouth's rebellion. Surrounding a fine Georgian mansion now used as an agricultural college, **Kingston Maurward Gardens** (*middle*) include 35 acres of 18th century gardens with a lake, a walled Elizabethan garden and a number of other delightful areas separated by hedges, terraces and stone balustrades. Two miles south-west of Dorchester the massive Iron Age hill-fort of **Maiden Castle** (*bottom*) dominates the landscape for miles around. The site was first fortified about 300 BC and some 5,000 people could be contained within the earthen ramparts.

One of the finest of Dorset's many stately homes and manor houses, **Athelhampton Hall** (*right*) dates from the 15th century. It is surrounded by a series of gardens which include a dovecot, fishponds and the Great Court Garden with its pyramid-shaped yews.

Regarded as pioneers of the trades union movement, the Tolpuddle Martyrs were sentenced to transportation in 1834 for uniting to resist a reduction in their wages as farm-workers. The **Martyrs' Memorial** (*left*) is one of several monuments to the men in the village of Tolpuddle. This pretty thatched cottage (*bottom*) was the birthplace in 1840 of Thomas Hardy. Tucked away in the hamlet of **Higher Bockhampton**, it lies on the edge of the wild and primitive Dorset moorland which features in his novels as Egdon Heath.

Situated in a peaceful wooded valley, the unspoilt village of **Milton Abbas** (*right*) has a long curving street lined by ancient thatched cottages. The village was rebuilt in the 18th century when the first Earl of Dorchester, to protect his privacy at Milton Abbey, demolished the old houses which surrounded it and built this new village nearby. **Milton Abbey** (*below*) was a Benedictine monastery from the 10th century, but the fine abbey church dates from the 14th century.

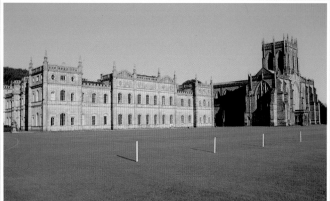

Evershot (*below*) is one of a number of delightful little villages south of Yeovil which nestle among wooded hills and are approached along winding lanes where wild flowers grow in profusion in spring and summer. Traditionally, cottages such as these beside the church are thatched with Dorset reed which gives a smoother finish than ordinary straw thatch.

Best known for its white hillside figure of the Cerne Giant, the village of **Cerne Abbas** is itself exceptionally beautiful. Its 10th century abbey was one of the most important in the south, but today only the gatehouse remains (*right*). There are many legends about the origins of the massive chalk figure (*above*), 180 feet from head to toe, which is carved into the hillside near the village. They include the possibilities that it is a fertility symbol, a representation of a local giant or a reference to Cromwell, who was often satirised as the "British Hercules".

Standing in the village of Godmanstone in the attractive Cerne Valley, the **Smith's Arms** (*left*) is a 17th century building of flint and stone which consists of a single room and is reputed to be the smallest inn in England. It is said that its first licence was given by King Charles II who stopped at the smithy to have his horse shod, and granted a licence so that he could also have a drink.

Weymouth and the Isle of Portland

With its long sweeping sandy bay and fine promenade, **Weymouth** (*above and right*) is one of the principal resorts on the south coast. Sea-bathing was first popularised here by George III who visited the town several times between 1789 and 1805. It quickly became a fashionable resort, as the many attractive late 18th and early 19th century terraces bear witness, and the coming of the railway further increased its popularity. Although it is no longer a major port, fishing boats and pleasure craft still mingle

with commercial vessels in the busy harbour, and ferries cross from here to the Channel Islands. Behind Weymouth on the downs is the famous **Osmington White Horse** (*left*). Of the many white horses seen on hillsides throughout southern England, this is amongst the most widely known. Cut into the chalk downland in the early 1800s, this huge equestrian representation of George III is the only white horse hill-figure in Britain to carry a rider.

Designated as a Site of Special Scientific Interest, the **Isle of Portland** is internationally important for its geology, its plant life and as an important site for the study of bird migration. Connected to the mainland only by a narrow neck of land, it was described by Thomas Hardy as "stretching out like the head of a bird into the English Channel". Portland is the source of the beautiful pale stone which has been used in such buildings as Buckingham Palace, St. Paul's Cathedral and the Cenotaph.

The peninsula culminates at **Portland Bill** (*below*) where strong tidal currents combined with submerged rocks make this part of the coast particularly hazardous to shipping. The 136-feet-high lighthouse which warns ships away from dangerous channels was built in 1903-06. An earlier lighthouse (*above*), built in 1789, is now used as a bird observatory. Scattered around the headland there are a number of strange rock tablets and formations. One of the largest and most curious of these, **Pulpit Rock** (*left*) stands off the west coast of the peninsula.

West Dorset

Formed over many thousands of years, **Chesil Beach** (*right*) is a remarkable bank of shingle that stretches some ten miles from Abbotsbury to the Isle of Portland. More than 40 feet high in places, this bank creates a remarkable natural breakwater on which the pebbles are inexplicably graded in size from west to east. **Abbotsbury** (*bottom*) is an ancient village of thatched, stone-built houses situated in a valley of outstanding natural beauty at the western end of Chesil Beach. Best known for its swannery, it has a number of fine buildings including a 15th century tithe barn which is one of the largest and finest in the country. Formerly a granary, it once contained a water-mill within its walls and now houses a country museum.

The **Subtropical Gardens** at Abbotsbury (*left*) were established in 1765 as a kitchen garden for the Countess of Ilchester. They now cover some twenty acres filled with rare and exotic plants from all over the world which flourish in the micro-climate created by their proximity to the sea. Famous for flowering trees and shrubs such as camellias, magnolias, rhododendrons and hydrangeas, the gardens are a mixture of formal and informal planting with shaded walks and spectacular vistas.

Easily reached along a pleasant coastal path from Bridport or West Bay is **Burton Bradstock** (*right*), a delightfully unspoiled example of a rural Dorset village. Its narrow, twisting lanes are lined with picturesque thatched cottages which make the village an immense attraction for artists and visitors from the nearby resorts. From the village a lane leads to a little beach backed by cliffs.

There are superb coastal views from Burton Cliff (*left*) which extend as far as Portland Bill and take in the remarkable Chesil bank. Fossils such as ammonites and belemnites can be found here, but care has to be taken because of the danger of rock falls.

The famous **Abbotsbury Swannery** (*right*) stands behind Chesil Beach on the long strip of water known as The Fleet. Swans were first kept here 600 years ago to provide fresh food for the nearby abbey, and this is now the only managed nesting colony of mute swans in Britain. Consisting of more than five hundred birds, the colony is best seen in April or May when the cygnets are first taking to the water.

The popular little resort of **West Bay** (*above*) faces the great sweep of Lyme Bay, and the harbour (*below*) was built at the mouth of the River Brit in 1740 to serve inland Bridport. In the 19th century this was a busy shipbuilding port where schooners and naval vessels continued to be built until 1879; now it provides a haven for small boats.

The impressive cliffs around West Bay are worn into a series of ledges by the effect of erosion on the alternating bands of hard and soft rock. About two miles north of West Bay is the ancient town of **Bridport** (*above*). It was famous for its rope-making industry, to which it owes the width of its thoroughfares which were used as rope-walks. The 18th century Town Hall, which overlooks the cross-roads in the centre of the town, is a pleasing building of Georgian design. Bridport appears in several of Hardy's novels where he calls the town Port Bredy.

The village of **Seatown** (*right*), with its beach of golden sand and shingle, is reached by a lane from the nearby village of Chideock. The beach is a favourite haunt of fishermen who catch both mackerel and bass here. The bay is backed by high sandstone cliffs which, although rugged in appearance, are subject to constant erosion by the wind and waves. The conical shape of **Colmer's Hill** (*below*) rises up behind the village of Symondsbury, west of Bridport. Although it is only 400 feet above sea-level, the hill, crowned with a group of windswept pine trees, is a distinctive landmark and a popular subject for artists and photographers. It was named after the Rev. John Colmer, who was rector in the early 19th century, but the trees were not planted on the top of the hill until around the time of the First World War. Between West Bay and Charmouth the smooth grassy downland, criss-crossed by hedgerows and clumps of gorse, meets the cliffs which provide an impressive backdrop for Lyme Bay. Here the glowing sandstone peak of **Golden Cap** (*below*) is the highest point on England's southern coast, reaching a height of 626 feet.

Set below steep hills overlooking the wide sweep of Lyme Bay, **Lyme Regis** (*above*) nestles in an Area of Outstanding Natural Beauty at the heart of the Jurassic Coast. This elegant old town, with its twisting, narrow streets, dignified Georgian houses and attractive promenade, is well known for its spectacular natural beauty. It can date its origins to 774 AD when the King of the West Saxons granted local monks the right to extract salt from sea water. It was under Edward I,

who used Lyme as a base for his wars against France, that "Regis" was added to its name. During the 18th century the town became a fashionable seaside resort and was a favourite place of Jane Austen who set part of her novel *Persuasion* in the town. No longer a commercial port, the attractive harbour is still a bustling scene of activity, well used by fishing boats and private craft. It is protected by the 14th century stone breakwater which is known as The Cobb (*left*).

The attractive little resort of **Charmouth** (*right*) is built on a steep hill which slopes down to a sand and shingle beach. It is sheltered by high cliffs which became a famous hunting ground for fossil collectors after the first complete ichthyosaurus fossil was found here by a local girl in 1811. The area is now part of an extensive nature reserve.

Delightfully situated in a natural amphitheatre sheltered by the surrounding hills, **Beaminster** (*left*) lies in an Area of Outstanding Natural Beauty. Here a row of handsome old cottages stand near the church which is held to be one of the best in the county. Redolent with all the charm of rural Dorset, **Powerstock** (*below*) is another charming village, built in terraces on the side of the hill. A maze of lanes winds through the village overlooked by the partly Norman church and flanked by stone cottages and fine houses.

In the north-western corner of the county near Beaminster is **Forde Abbey** (*below*). It was originally a 12th century Cistercian foundation but much restoration and additional building was undertaken by the last abbot of Forde in the 1520s before work was halted by the dissolution of the monasteries. In the 17th century, Forde Abbey was converted into a private house, and a fine park with lawns, ponds and gardens was laid out.

North Dorset and the Stour Valley

A town of considerable historical and architectural interest, **Sherborne** is set amongst green hills on the River Yeo. There are many notable old buildings in the town including the outstanding Abbey Church (*below*). Sherborne Abbey was founded in 998 but the present structure dates mainly from the 15th century. A fine Saxon doorway remains from the earlier building, as well as a tenor bell given to the abbey by Cardinal Wolsey. At the foot of Cheap Street is a 14th century conduit (*right*) which was once a wash-house and stood within the cloisters of the Abbey Church.

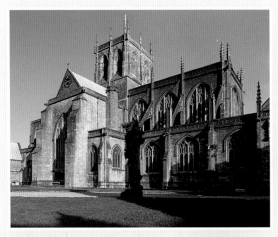

The most northerly town in Dorset, **Gillingham** (*right*) is a thriving and attractive market town with a fascinating history. From the Stone Age onwards there have been settlements here, and in the Middle Ages Gillingham was the seat of a royal hunting lodge. John Constable, England's best-known landscape painter, visited Gillingham on several occasions and some of his paintings of the area, including Old Gillingham Bridge, now hang in London's Tate Gallery.

The market town of **Shaftesbury** (*left*) is rich in history and one of its most famous and picturesque landmarks is Gold Hill. This ancient cobbled street, lined with pretty tiled and thatched cottages, leads steeply down from the present day High Street and affords magnificent views over Blackmoor Vale. The first recorded reference to Gold Hill was in 1362.

Blandford Forum (*right*) was largely destroyed by fire in 1731 and the rebuilt town is an outstanding example of classical Georgian architecture. The imposing buildings which surround the market place owe their handsome appearance to two brothers who were local builders. **Sturminster Newton** (*below*) is a particularly attractive village. The Old Mill stands in a beautiful setting on the banks of the River Stour, which is spanned by a fine medieval bridge.

Originally founded as a nunnery in 713, beautiful **Wimborne Minster** (*right*) dominates the peaceful market town of Wimborne which lies in the east of the county between the Rivers Stour and Avon. Rebuilt in the 12th century, the Minster embraces many architectural styles and among its many items of historic interest are an astronomical clock believed to date from 1325, a notable chained library and a quarter-jack in the form of a grenadier which strikes the bell on the west tower marking the quarter hours.

Near Wimborne Minster are **Badbury Rings**, a vast triple-banked Iron Age hill-fort which is a notable local landmark. A magnificent avenue of trees (*left*) lines the road just below the Rings. Legend has it that the farmer who planted them intended there to be one tree for each day of the year on the two-mile stretch. Built in the 1660s, **Kingston Lacy** (*below*) is a magnificent country house standing in extensive grounds. Considerably altered in the 19th century by Sir Charles Barry, designer of the Houses of Parliament, it contains a fine art collection.

The large parish church and handsome brick-and-timber houses which line the main street testify to the former status of **Cranborne** (*top*). It is now a peaceful village surrounded by beautiful rolling countryside, but from the 10th to the 12th centuries it was the location of the Chase Court which controlled hunting in the nearby royal forest of Cranborne Chase and was important enough to have its own grammar school, abbey and medieval manor house. Just outside Wimborne, the ancient village of **Pamphill** (*middle*) was the estate village for Kingston Lacy. It lies in the midst of unspoilt countryside and is known for the quantity and quality of its fine brick-and-timber houses as well as a charming group of sturdy cottages, with thick walls and neatly thatched roofs, which adjoin the picturesque green. A superb avenue of oak trees, planted in 1846, leads to Pamphill church.

The ruins of a Norman church stand in isolation within the central circle of prehistoric **Knowlton Rings** (*bottom*). Originally consisting of three circular henges, Knowlton was constructed about 4,000 years ago, and is one of the most significant ceremonial sites remaining from neolithic times. It was probably used for religious purposes, and human sacrifices may have taken place here. It is thought that the church was built at this spot to emphasise the power of Christianity over pagan beliefs.

Poole and Bournemouth

Overlooking Poole Harbour, the beautiful gardens at **Compton Acres** (*right*) were begun in 1919 and are reputed to be some of the finest in Europe. The delightful Italian Garden, with its fountains and water-lilies, has a particularly tranquil atmosphere. Situated at the entrance to Poole Harbour, the superb beach at **Sandbanks** (*below*) is popular with yachtsmen and windsurfers as well as holiday-makers.

Situated on one of the largest shallow-water anchorages in Britain, **Poole** (*left*) has always been an important port and it is now also a popular resort with fine parks and sandy beaches. The heart of the town centres around the harbour where there are numerous buildings of historic interest including the splendid Custom House. The third custom house on this site, it was built in 1813 after the previous one burned down.

Situated between the bustling resorts of Poole and Bournemouth, on a three-mile-long stretch of golden sands, are the popular little seaside resorts of **Branksome Chine** (*top*) and **Canford Cliffs** (*middle*). Backed by low cliffs which are divided by wooded chines, they offer safe bathing and are popular for boating activities.

Located to the west of Bournemouth's central beach, **Durley Chine** (*below*) is one of several wooded chines which cut a path through the cliffs. It leads down to a golden, sandy beach which is popular for family holidays with its safe bathing and good facilities for children. The additional attractions of Bournemouth pier can be reached by a short walk along the promenade.

Situated in the centre of the wide sweep of Poole Bay facing the English Channel, **Bournemouth** is one of the country's leading resorts. With its superb sandy beaches, it is a popular location for family holidays. Bournemouth is also known for its wooded chines and splendid gardens which include more than 1,700 acres of spacious parks and gardens. Along with the Lower and Upper Gardens, the colourful Central Gardens (*right*) extend along the little Bourne valley to the seafront. The famous Pavilion was built in 1929 and contains a theatre, a ballroom and a restaurant.

The resort's earliest pier, replacing a wooden jetty, was built in 1861, and the present iron structure opened in 1880. A bandstand was added five years later, while more recent additions have included a leisure complex, shops, an amusement arcade and a show bar. Situated in the heart of the town, the prestigious International Centre (*below*) hosts conferences, exhibitions and a variety of entertainments.

Situated just east of Bournemouth, the little resort of **Southbourne** (*above*) has a sand and shingle beach sheltered by steep cliffs. To the east, the promontory of Hengistbury Head can be seen curving around Christchurch harbour. The Head is a popular observation point for bird migrations. From Bournemouth, the sands, promenade and cliff drive extend eastwards to **Boscombe** (*below*). Although it is smaller than its neighbour, Boscombe is a popular resort in its own right with fine sands, splendid gardens and a 750-feet-long pier which first opened in 1889. Along this part of the coast the cliffs are carved by a series of steep valleys, or chines, through which paths zigzag down to the sea. Colourful gardens line Boscombe Chine providing a shady alternative to the seafront.

Around Christchurch

Situated between the estuaries of the Rivers Avon and Stour, **Christchurch** (*right*) has a sheltered harbour which offers safe moorings for yachts and other small boats. Originally one of King Alfred's walled strongholds against the Danes, Christchurch is a tranquil town which takes its name from its 11th century priory church standing behind the quay. This magnificent building was begun in 1094 and took four centuries to complete. The Priory Church, at just over 300 feet, is England's longest parish church and contains many fine carvings and monuments. The village of **Mudeford** (*below*) has the advantage of facing both Christchurch harbour and the coast where there is the long sandy sweep of Avon Beach. Fishing boats are launched at the busy quay where lobster pots and fishing tackle can often be seen.

From here there are fine views along the coast and also south-eastwards to the jagged points of The Needles on the Isle of Wight. Eastwards from Mudeford is the popular resort of Highcliffe-on-Sea where steps lead up from the beach through 100-feet-high cliffs to **Highcliffe Castle** (*bottom*). Built in the 1830s for Lord Stuart de Rothesay, a distinguished diplomat in the reign of George IV, this Grade I listed building is an outstanding example of the Romantic Picturesque style of architecture and contains some unique medieval stonework.